It's fun to draw
Knights, Castles, and Pirates

It's fun to draw
Knights, Castles, and Pirates

Mark Bergin

Sky Pony Press
New York

Author:

Mark Bergin was born in Hastings, England. He has illustrated an award-winning series and written over twenty books. He has done many book designs, layouts, and storyboards in many styles including cartoon for numerous books, posters, and adverts. He lives in Bexhill-on-Sea with his wife and three children.

HOW TO USE THIS BOOK:

Start by following the numbered splats on the left-hand page. These steps will ask you to add some lines to your drawing. The new lines are always drawn in red so you can see how the drawing builds from step to step. Read the "You can do it!" splats to learn about drawing and shading techniques you can use.

Sky Pony Press books may be purchased in bulk at special discounts for sales promotion, corporate gifts, fund-raising, or educational purposes. Special editions can also be created to specifications. For details, contact the Special Sales Department, Sky Pony Press, 307 West 36th Street, 11th Floor, New York, NY 10018 or info@ skyhorsepublishing.com.

Sky Pony® is a registered trademark of Skyhorse Publishing, Inc.®, a Delaware corporation.

Visit our website at www.skyponypress.com.

10 9 8 7 6 5 4 3 2 1

This product conforms to CPSIA 2008

Library of Congress Cataloging-in-Publication Data is available on file.

Cover design by Daniel Brount
Cover illustration by Mark Bergin
ISBN: 978-1-5107-4361-8
Printed in China

Contents

Contents

It's fun to draw

Knights, Castles, and Pirates

Castle guard

1 Start with the helmet. Add eye slots and dots for breathing holes.

2 Add a shield. Draw in markings.

you can do it!
Use a black felt-tip marker for the lines and add color using watercolor paint.

3 Draw a rectangle for the body, and add legs.

4 Add the arm holding a spear.

5 Draw in a belt and a scabbard.

Splat-a-fact!
Important knights lived in castles.

Eagleford Castle

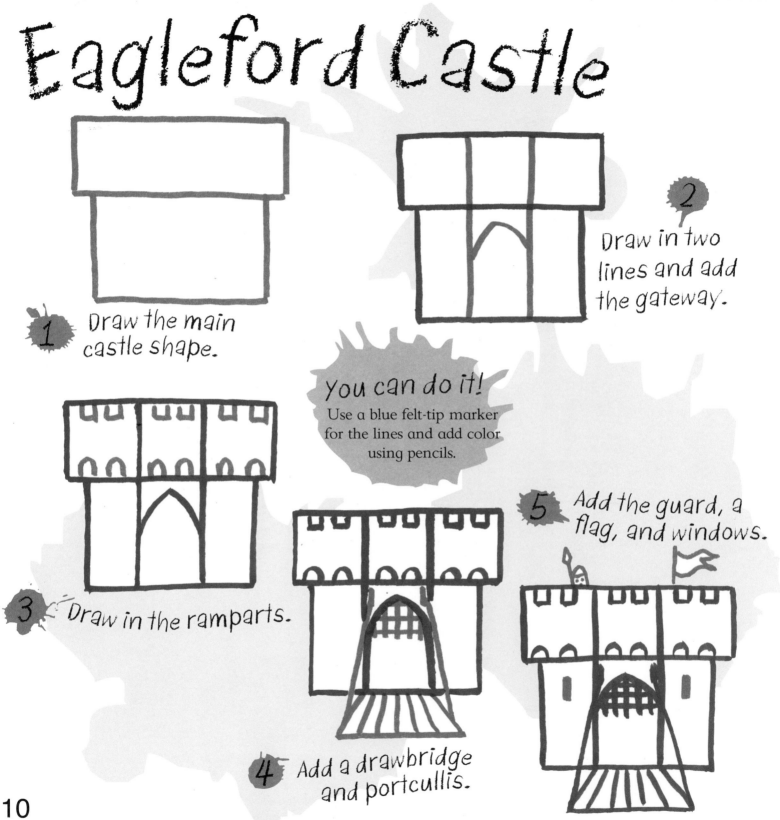

1 Draw the main castle shape.

2 Draw in two lines and add the gateway.

you can do it!
Use a blue felt-tip marker for the lines and add color using pencils.

3 Draw in the ramparts.

4 Add a drawbridge and portcullis.

5 Add the guard, a flag, and windows.

splat-a-fact!
The moat and drawbridge kept the castle safe from enemies.

11

Norman knight

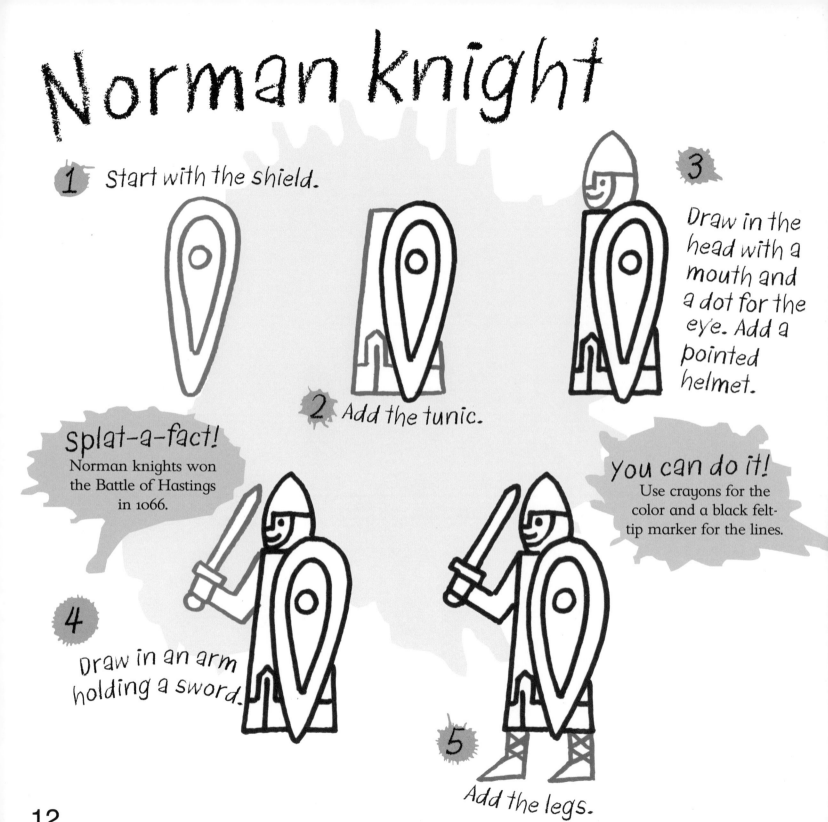

1 Start with the shield.

2 Add the tunic.

3 Draw in the head with a mouth and a dot for the eye. Add a pointed helmet.

Splat-a-fact!
Norman knights won the Battle of Hastings in 1066.

4 Draw in an arm holding a sword.

you can do it!
Use crayons for the color and a black felt-tip marker for the lines.

5 Add the legs.

12

Axe knight

1 Cut out a helmet. Draw a slit and breathing holes. Glue down onto colored paper.

2 Cut out a tunic from white paper. Glue down.

3 Now tear out the shield shape and glue down. Tear out a red cross and add to the shield.

Splat-a-fact!

Knights could fight with an axe or just throw it at the enemy.

you can do it!

Cut out the knight's armor shapes from tin foil. Use a marker for the details.

4 Cut out legs. Glue down. Add detail.

5 Cut out an arm and the axe head. Cut out the handle. Glue down. Add details.

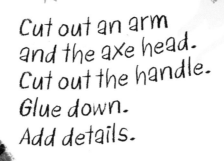

MAKE SURE YOU GET AN ADULT TO HELP YOU WHEN USING SCISSORS!

14

15

Archer

1 Start with the head. Add a helmet, a mouth, and a dot for the eye.

2 Add the body and arms.

3 Draw in a curved bow. Add an arrow.

4 Add a quiver and belt.

5 Draw in the legs and feet. Finish details.

You can do it!
Use crayons for all textures and paint over with watercolors. Sponge on some of the inks to create added interest.

Splat-a-fact!
Archers stood on top of battlements and shot at the enemy.

17

Ravenswood Castle

1 Start with a square and add a gateway.

2 Draw in the towers and add windows.

you can do it!
Use a soft pencil for the lines and add color using watercolor paint.

splat-a-fact!
The main gate was very strong. It was a thick, iron-studded, wooden door.

3 Draw in triangles for the pointed roofs.

4 Add finishing details: windows, doors, and battlements.

Jousting tent

1 Start with the tent top. Add a wavy line.

2 Draw in the tent with a gap for the entrance.

you can do it!
Use a black felt-tip marker for the lines and add color using colored felt-tip markers.

Splat-a-fact!
The knight's jousting tent was where he got ready for the tournament.

3 Add stripes and a flag.

4 Draw the knight's colors on the flag and banner.

Jousting knight

1 Start with the horse's head and body.

2 Add the eyes, nostrils, and hooves.

3 Draw in the knight with a helmet. Add his legs on either side of the horse.

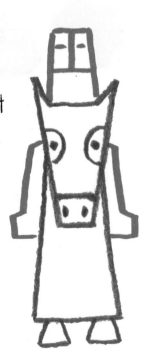

4 Add a lance and shield. Draw feathers on the helmet.

Splat-a-fact!
It took about 14 years to train to be a knight.

The joust

1 Start with the horse's head and surcoat.

2 Add its eyes, mouth, tail, and hooves.

you can do it!
Use a brown felt-tip marker for the lines and add color with colored felt-tip markers.

3 Draw in the knight with a shield.

4 Draw in the reins and a saddle. Add detail to the surcoat.

5 Add a lance. Add a feather on the helmet.

splat-a-fact!
A knight needed lots of money—a shiny suit of armor was very expensive.

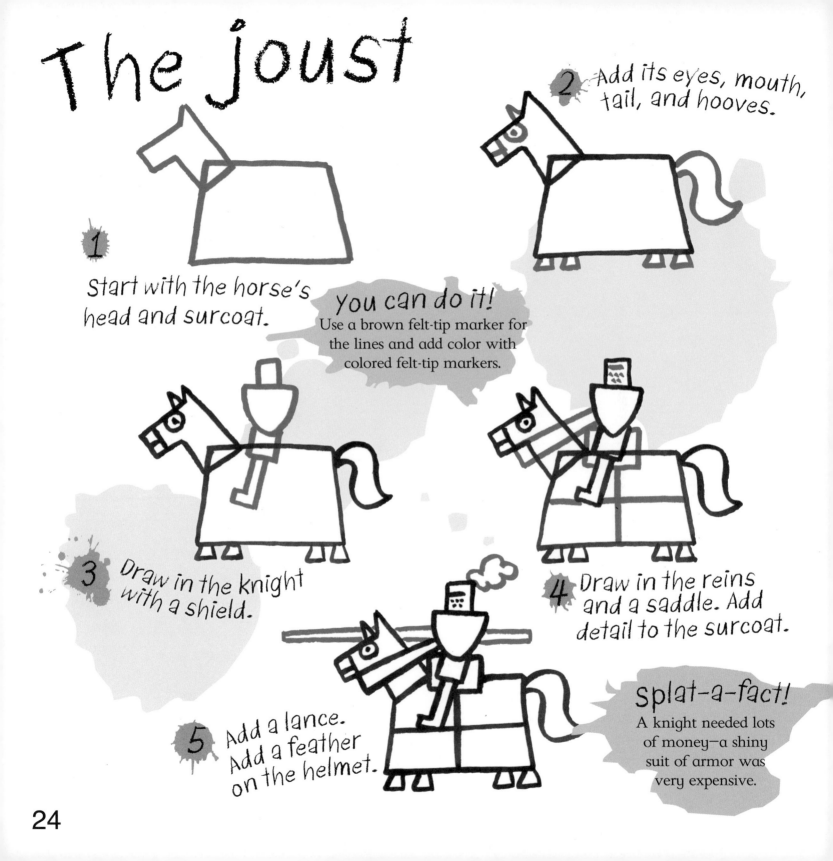

Mace knight

1 Start with the helmet shape. Add a visor with dots for breathing holes and two slits for the eyes.

2 Add the knight's tunic and shield.

3 Add a belt and the legs.

4 Draw in the arm holding a mace.

Hawkbury Castle

1 Cut out the middle section of the castle. Glue down.

2 Cut out two towers. Glue down.

you can do it!

Cut out the shapes from colored paper. Glue these onto a sheet of blue paper. Use felt-tip markers for the lines.

3 Draw in windows and a doorway.

4 Add a guard and a large banner on top.

MAKE SURE YOU GET AN ADULT TO HELP YOU WHEN USING SCISSORS!

splat-a-fact!
The walls of a castle were very high to stop attackers from climbing in.

Arabian knight

1 Start with the tunic and a round shield. Add details.

2 Add the head, with dots for the eyes, a nose, and a moustache.

3 Add the helmet shape.

you can do it!
Use crayons to create textures and paint over with watercolor paint. Use a soft pencil for the lines.

4 Draw in an arm holding a curved sword.

5 Add the scabbard. Draw in the legs.

splat-a-fact!
Arabian knights had to fight in the desert. It was important that they had water to drink between battles.

Spearman

1 Start with the helmet and the head. Add dots for the eyes and a mouth.

2 Add the tunic.

3 Draw in the arm and spear.

you can do it!
Use a brown felt-tip marker for the lines and add color with soft, chalky pastels. Smudge and blend some of the colors to add interest.

splat-a-fact!
In battle, the spearman could keep enemies at a safe distance with his long spear.

4 Add a long shield shape.

5 Draw in the legs.

Battling knight

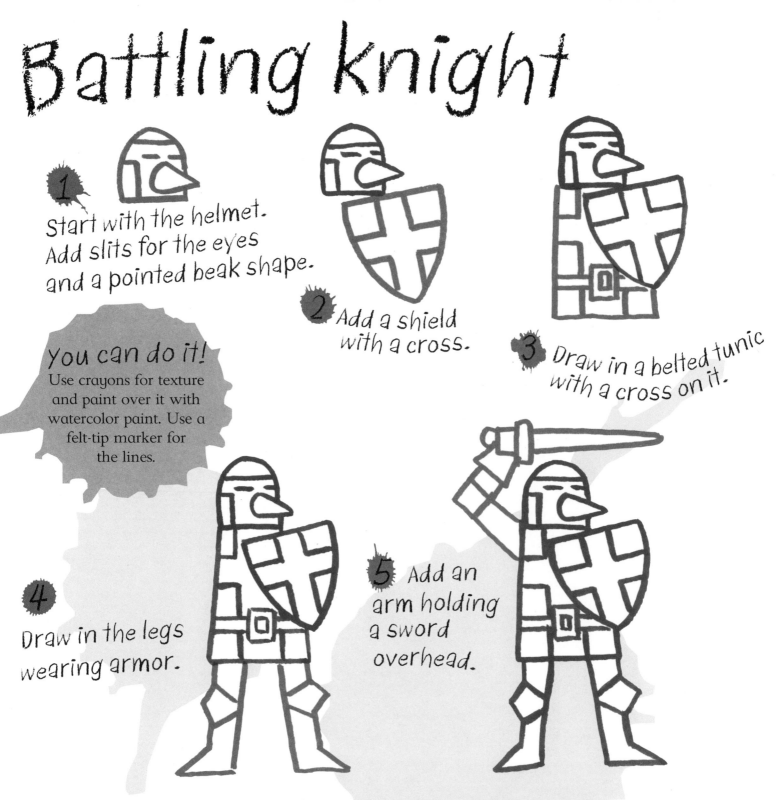

1 Start with the helmet. Add slits for the eyes and a pointed beak shape.

2 Add a shield with a cross.

3 Draw in a belted tunic with a cross on it.

you can do it!
Use crayons for texture and paint over it with watercolor paint. Use a felt-tip marker for the lines.

4 Draw in the legs wearing armor.

5 Add an arm holding a sword overhead.

splat-a-fact!
A knight's suit of armor had to be built to fit him exactly.

Barnacle Boris

1 Start with an oval for the head, and add a line and ears.

2 Add a hat, nose, mouth, eyes, and eyebrows.

3 Draw in the body. Add two lines for the waistcoat.

4 Draw in the trousers, belt, and feet.

Splat-a-fact!
Pirates used guns and swords as weapons.

5 Draw in arms holding a pistol and a sword.

Use crayons to create various textures, then paint over it with watercolor paint. Use a felt-tip marker for the lines.

37

Sharktooth Jack

1 Draw in the head shape. Add a line for the headscarf.

3 Draw in the body.

you can do it!
Use a crayon to draw the clouds. To add texture paint over with watercolor paint. Use a felt-tip marker for the lines.

2 Draw in the eyes, brows, and mouth. Add dots for stubble and a knotted headscarf.

splat-a-fact!
Pirates buried their treasure on desert islands.

4 Add ragged trousers and legs.

5 Draw in the arms and hands. Draw in the spade.

Redbeard

1 Draw in the head shape. Add a line for the headscarf.

2 Draw in the beard and eye patch. Add dots for the eye and mouth.

3 Draw in a circle for the body. Add a belt and waistcoat.

4 Draw in two arms and a lit match.

5 Draw in ragged trousers, and add the feet.

you can do it!
Use a graphite pencil for the lines and colored inks to add color.

splat-a-fact!
Pirate ships had cannons to shoot at their enemies with.

Scurvy Jim

1 Draw in the head shape. Add a line for the headscarf.

Splat-a-fact!

Pirate treasure is kept in a wooden chest.

2 Draw a dot for the eye. Add the mouth, ear, hair, and knotted headscarf.

3 Draw in the body shape, and add a belt and waistcoat.

4 Draw in the arms carrying a treasure chest and sword.

5 Draw in ragged trousers, and add the feet.

42

you can do it!
Use a black felt-tip marker for the lines. Add color using oil pastels and draw scribbly lines so the color looks more interesting.

43

squid lips sid

you can do it!
Place your paper over different surfaces and use color pencils to create interesting textures. Use a felt-tip marker for the lines.

1 Start with the head shape, and draw a line for the headscarf.

2 Add dots for eyes. Draw in the eyebrows, an ear, and the knotted headscarf.

3 Add the body, arms, and hands.

4 Draw in the torn trousers and feet.

5 Draw in the belt and broom.

44

45

Starboard Steve

1 Start with the head shape. Draw in a line for the headscarf.

Splat-a-fact!
"X" marks the spot on a treasure map where the treasure is buried.

2 Draw in the eyes, mouth, and hair. Add an ear, an earring, and a knotted headscarf.

3 Add a box-shaped body and two lines for the waistcoat.

4 Draw in torn trousers, and add feet.

5 Draw in the arms holding a treasure map. Add a neckerchief.

you can do it!

Use felt-tip markers for the lines. Add color using oil pastels. Blend or smudge with your fingers.

Monkey

1 Draw two overlapping circles for the head. Add the hairline.

2 Draw in dots for the eyes and nostrils. Add a mouth and ears.

3 Draw in the body. Add a headscarf.

you can do it!
Cut out strips of corrugated cardboard for the rope and glue down torn tissue paper for the background.

4 Draw in torn trousers, and add the monkey's legs and feet.

5 Add arms and a long tail. Draw circles for fingers.

Captain Clunk

MAKE SURE YOU GET AN ADULT TO HELP YOU WHEN USING SCISSORS!

1. Start by cutting out this shape for the pirate's jacket. Glue down.

2. Cut out the face shape. Glue down. Use a felt-tip marker to draw in buttons, hair, a nose, and an eye patch.

you can do it!

As you cut out each shape from colored paper or tin foil, glue it down.

3. Cut out the pirate's hat and beard from black paper. Glue down. Cut out a boot and a peg leg from brown paper. Glue down.

4. Cut out the sword from tin foil and glue down. Cut out hands and glue down. Cut a crutch from brown paper and glue down.

50

splat-a-fact!
Some pirates had wooden legs.

Sophie Storm

1 Start with a circle for the head. Add a nose, mouth, and eyes.

2 Draw in a hat and hair.

3 Draw in a box-shaped body. Add sleeves.

you can do it!
Use a brown felt-tip marker for the lines and add color with colored crayons.

4 Draw in circles for the hands holding a sword and dagger. Add belts and buckles.

splat-a-fact!
Sometimes girls were pirates, too!

5 Add the trousers and the feet.

One-eyed John

1 Start with an oval for the head. Add ears.

2 Draw in a headscarf. Add a nose, a dot for the eye, an eye patch, and a dagger between his teeth.

3 Draw in a box-shaped body. Add a waistcoat and buckle.

4 Draw in the arms with circles for the hands. Add a pistol.

Splat-a-fact!
Pirates wore eye patches and headscarves.

5 Draw in ragged trousers, and add the feet.

Pete the Plank

1 Start by drawing in the head shape with a line for the headscarf.

2 Add a mouth, an ear, eyebrows, and dots for eyes. Draw in a knotted headscarf.

3 Draw in the body. Add a belt and buckle.

splat-a-fact!
Pirates climbed the "rigging"—ropes that controlled the mast.

you can do it!
Use a brown felt-tip marker for the outlines and color in with different felt-tip markers.

4 Draw in ragged trousers, and add the feet.

5 Draw in the arms and hands. Add stripes to the trousers and shirt.

Sharkbait George

1 Start with the head shape. Add a line for the headscarf.

2 Draw in the knotted headscarf. Add an ear, mouth, and an arrow-shaped closed eye.

3 Add the ragged trousers.

4 Draw in the arms, with one holding up a telescope.

you can do it!
Use a felt-tip marker for the lines and then add color with watercolor paints. Dab on more color with a sponge to add texture.

Splat-a-fact!
Telescopes helped pirates see into the distance.

5 Draw in a waistcoat, buckle, and belt. Add the legs, feet, and a cannonball.

Gunpowder Billy

1 Start with an oval for the head. Add a line for the headscarf.

2 Add a mouth, nose, hair, and dots for the eyes. Draw in the knotted headscarf.

3 Draw in the body shape.

splat-a-fact!

Pirates attacked enemy ships and kept much of the loot.

you can do it!

Use a felt-tip marker for the lines. Add color using chalky pastels. Use your fingers to blend the colors.

4 Draw in the ragged trousers, and add legs and feet.

5 Draw in the arms, a treasure chest, and a bag of loot.

Captain Black

1 Start with a square-shaped head. Add the shape of the hat.

2 Draw in the nose, hair, and beard.

3 Draw in one eye, an eye patch, and a mouth. Add a box-shaped body and an "X" to the hat.

you can do it!
Using crayons to create texture, paint over it with watercolor paint. Use a felt-tip marker for the lines.

Splat-a-fact!
Some pirates had hooks for hands.

4 Draw in the jacket details: buttons and button holes. Add buckle. Draw in boots.

5 Draw in sleeves with big cuffs. Add one hand with a sword and one with a hook.

62

Index